TASTES LIKE MUSIC

17 QUIRKS OF THE BRAIN AND BODY

BY
Maria Birmingham

ILLUSTRATED BY
Monika Melnychuk

Owl kids

For Mom and Dad—With love and gratitude
—MB

For Madelyn and Molly
—MM

Text © 2014 Maria Birmingham
Illustrations © 2014 Monika Melnychuk

Owlkids Books acknowledges the financial support of the Canada Council for the Arts, the Ontario Arts Council, the Government of Canada through the Canada Book Fund (CBF) and the Government of Ontario through the Ontario Media Development Corporation's Book Initiative for our publishing activities.

Published in Canada by
Owlkids Books Inc.
10 Lower Spadina Avenue
Toronto, ON M5V 2Z2

Published in the United States by
Owlkids Books Inc.
1700 Fourth Street
Berkeley, CA 94710

Library and Archives Canada Cataloguing in Publication

Birmingham, Maria, author
    Tastes like music : 17 quirks of the brain and body / written by Maria Birmingham ; illustrations by Monika Melnychuk.

Includes index.
ISBN 978-1-77147-010-0 (bound).--ISBN 978-1-77147-083-4 (pbk.)

    1. Brain--Diseases--Juvenile literature. 2. Cognition disorders--Juvenile literature. 3. Neurology--Juvenile literature. I. Melnychuk, Monika, illustrator II. Title.

RC386.2.B57 2014   j616.8   C2014-900386-2

Library of Congress Control Number: 2014931870

Edited by: John Crossingham and Jessica Burgess
Designed by: Alisa Baldwin and Barb Kelly

Manufactured in Dongguan, China, in April 2014, by Toppan Leefung Packaging & Printing (Dongguan) Co., Ltd.
Job #BAYDC8

A   B   C   D   E   F

 Publisher of Chirp, chickaDEE and OWL
www.owlkidsbooks.com

Tastes Like Music

INTRODUCTION — 4

TAKE A WALK DOWN MEMORY LANE — 6

YOU SNOOZE, YOU...WALK? — 8

BENT OUT OF SHAPE — 10

LIVING LOST — 12

THAT'S NOT MUSIC TO MY EARS — 14

THE TALE OF THE TONGUE — 16

THAT SOUND IN YOUR HEAD — 18

THE WORLD IN TECHNICOLOR — 20

DOWN THE RABBIT HOLE — 22

PLACE THAT FACE — 24

MY, WHAT A LOT OF TEETH YOU HAVE! — 26

IT'S HAIR-RAISING — 28

MAKING SENSE OF IT — 30

I SAW THE LIGHT...AND SNEEZED — 32

PRINT-FREE PEOPLE — 34

PEOPLE POWER — 36

THE NOSE DOESN'T KNOW — 38

INDEX — 40

This Is What Human Looks Like

We humans are a complicated bunch. In some ways, we are a lot alike. Generally, we each have two eyes, a nose, a mouth, two ears, and so on. And we all behave pretty similarly, too. Every single member of the human race laughs, cries, burps, sneezes, sleeps—you get the picture.

Of course, on the flip side, we're also all unique—from the color of our eyes and the sound of our laugh to the talents and memories we each have.

But a few people take their unique qualities to another level entirely—they have abilities or traits that will amaze you. Some can contort their bodies in ways that are impossible for the rest of us. Others have a sense of sight that allows them to see colors invisible to just about everyone else on Earth. And a select few don't have the slightest trace of a fingerprint.

These traits and abilities—and many others like them—fascinate scientists as they try to understand the mysteries of the human body. Each one has helped experts learn more about the body, and they have all shown us that we have a lot to learn about what it means to be human. As you wind your way through these pages, you'll get a look at the science of how our bodies and brains work. Along the way, you'll see what makes each of us so similar and so completely different—all at the same time!

Take a Walk Down MEMORY Lane

Have you ever had one of those days that you'd rather forget? For people with highly superior autobiographical memory (HSAM), forgetting the past is practically impossible. They can recall almost every single day of their lives since the time they were about ten years old. Ask them what they were wearing on March 4, 2009, and people with HSAM will remember everything down to the smallest of details—right down to the color of their socks—without having to rack their brains.

TOTAL RECALL

HSAM was first documented in 2006. At the moment, there are only about fifty people on the planet known to have this incredible knack for remembering. In July 2012, researchers at the University of California, Irvine, studied eleven people with HSAM and found that the front and middle parts of their brains are linked together differently than those without the condition. According to the lead researcher, Aurora LePort, there are stronger "white matter" connections between the two areas. (White matter is a tissue that controls the signals passed between regions of the brain.) The study suggests these stronger connections give those with HSAM a sharper memory.

DON'T FORGET!

People with HSAM don't necessarily have a top-notch memory when it comes to basic short-term memorization, such as remembering details in a picture or playing a card-matching game. But there's no denying they outdo everyone else in their ability to recall the details of their lives. This may be because short-term memory and long-term memory involve different brain regions. While the prefrontal cortex at the very front of the brain stores short-term memories, long-term memories are stored in many different areas throughout the brain.

WHAT'S IT LIKE?

Nicole Donohue of Morris Township, New Jersey, has known since she was twelve that her memory is exceptional. But she didn't know there was a name for her extraordinary ability until she was an adult.

SHORT—TERM VS. LONG—TERM MEMORY

SHORT-TERM MEMORIES generally last about twenty to thirty seconds. The information is not stored in your brain, since it's only needed in the moment to perform a specific task. Once used, the memory fades.

LONG-TERM MEMORIES can last for decades. These memories are divided into three categories:

- **Episodic memory** is the recollection of an event, like your sixth birthday party or the first day of school.

- **Semantic memory** involves ideas, facts, language, and knowledge. It's what helps you picture a familiar object, like a bicycle, when your friend mentions it during a conversation.

- **Procedural memory** has to do with remembering how to perform an action or a skill, such as riding a bike.

How would you explain what goes on in your mind when you are recalling a day that's years in the past?

I can usually remember details such as what the weather was like that day, what day of the week it was, what I ate that day, and what songs I listened to. I can usually recall these details with ease, but some days are easier to remember than others, especially if something extremely positive or extremely negative happened.

Do memories constantly stream through your mind, or can you call them up when you want?

Memories are constantly streaming through my mind. It is usually extremely difficult to turn them off, so to speak.

Some people with the condition say it's haunting to have this type of memory. How do you feel about having HSAM?

Usually I do not mind having HSAM, but it can be somewhat frustrating and overstimulating at times to have memories constantly running through my mind. Also, some people do not understand why I still feel so emotional about events that happened many years ago. When you have HSAM, the emotions associated with memories usually stay as raw as they were when the events first happened.

What are the advantages and disadvantages of HSAM?

It is extremely helpful when memorizing material for exams, and it is easy to remember positive things that have happened to me. The disadvantages are that it is nearly impossible to forget mistakes I have made or negative things that have happened to me. Also, since there are so few people with HSAM, it can be difficult to relate to others at times.

You Snooze, You...Walk?

We all need some zzzz's. A good night's sleep gives the body time to rest and repair its cells and tissues. Some scientists suggest it also allows the brain to process information after a long day. Most people move around in bed as they sleep, but a few actually take a stroll. About 4 percent of adults sleepwalk on a regular basis. It's even more common in kids between the ages of five and twelve, although most outgrow the habit in their teens. While a sleepwalker generally just wanders around, some sleepwalkers perform activities, like texting, getting dressed or undressed, cooking, or even driving! Although a sleepwalker's eyes are open as she roams, she's not awake. And in the morning, she won't remember ever having left her bed.

ON THE MOVE

Sleepwalking usually occurs within a few hours of drifting off, in the deepest stages of sleep. (See the chart for sleep stages on the next page.) An episode can range from a few seconds to about half an hour, but most last for less than ten minutes. At that point, the sleepwalker typically returns to bed and remains there for the rest of the night. Sleepwalking usually isn't a cause for concern, and most people don't need treatment unless their safety becomes an issue.

SLIGHTLY SLEEPING

So why do some people sleepwalk? It's often assumed that sleepwalkers are acting out their dreams. But the body can't actually move during the dream stage of sleep. The scientific reason for sleepwalking is still uncertain. But sleep experts like Dr. Michel Cramer Bornemann believe there are occasional glitches with electrical signals within the brain. He thinks that when this happens, certain parts of the brain awaken slightly, while others remain asleep. Being in this state between sleep and wakefulness probably causes an episode of sleepwalking.

ZZZZZZZZ,

SLEEP STAGES

One complete sleep cycle lasts about ninety minutes, and within each cycle, there are five stages of sleep.

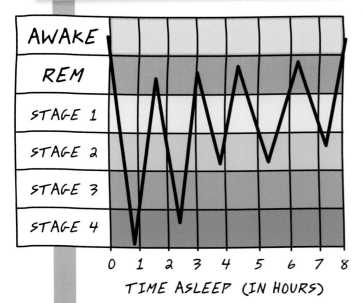

TIME ASLEEP (IN HOURS)

STAGE 1: During this light stage, your muscles relax and you start to drift off. You can be easily awakened at this point.

STAGE 2: Brain activity slows down, and so do your breathing and your heart rate. The body is getting ready to enter deep sleep.

STAGE 3: This is the start of deep sleep. If you are woken up now, you will be woozy and confused for a few minutes.

STAGE 4: You are in your deepest sleep of the night. It is difficult to wake someone up in this stage.

REM (STAGE 5): This stage is also known as REM—or rapid eye movement—sleep. Your eyes dart back and forth very quickly under the lids. Your brain is as active as it is when you're awake, and this is when most dreams happen. In this stage, your arms and legs are actually paralyzed.

WHAT TO DO WHEN SOMEONE IS SLEEPWALKING

Many people say that you should never wake a sleepwalker. But the truth is that a sleepwalker can be injured while he wanders, so you're actually doing him a favor by waking him. Experts do suggest, however, that it's best to gently guide a sleepwalker back to bed whenever possible. If you need to wake him, do it calmly—it's common for a sleepwalker to be confused for a few moments, since he's unsure about what's going on.

ZZZ

Bent Out of Shape

When you hear the term "double-jointed," it may stir up images of professional contortionists bent in ways that would make *your* body hurt. But this condition isn't always so extreme. More common examples of double-jointedness, or joint hypermobility, include bending your thumb back so it touches the wrist, making your elbow bend back past 180 degrees, or touching the floor with your palms without bending your knees. In spite of its name, double-jointedness doesn't mean that a person has two joints instead of one. It simply describes someone who can extend his joints farther than others can. The joints most commonly affected are fingers, wrists, elbows, and knees.

SOCKET TO YOU

Less than 5 percent of the adult population has joint hypermobility. It's more common in kids, although they often outgrow it as their joints tighten with age. The shape of your joints can determine if you are hypermobile. At a joint, two bones come together in a socket. Some people have deep sockets, while others have shallow ones. With a shallow socket, the bones can move more easily—this feature can make a person double-jointed. Some people are so flexible they can roll a bone out of the socket and roll it back into place!

WHAT A STRETCH

Another source of double-jointedness is your ligaments—these are the tough tissues that connect bones within the socket. These strong fibers also control how far your bones can move. Ligaments are made of a substance called collagen; some people are born with weaker collagen than others. When that's the case, ligaments will have the ability to stretch quite easily, and that can cause double-jointedness.

THE PROS AND CONS OF HAVING JOINT HYPERMOBILITY

Besides allowing you to shock your friends, double-jointedness has other benefits. For instance, a baseball pitcher who has double-jointed fingers will have an edge when he throws the ball, since he has an extra range of motion in his hands. And of course, double-jointed gymnasts have an easier time in their sport thanks to their increased flexibility. The condition can also help musicians—it's easier to play a guitar or a piano if you have double-jointed fingers. But double-jointedness also has its drawbacks. Because the joints can overstretch more easily, it often leads to joint pain, dislocations, fractures, and muscle strains.

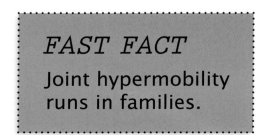

FAST FACT
Joint hypermobility runs in families.

JUST THE JOINTS

Here are some of the joints that help you get around from day to day.

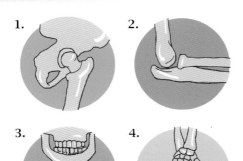

1. BALL AND SOCKET: This joint allows for forward, backward, and circular motion. Both your hip and your shoulder are ball-and-socket joints. Thanks to these joints, you can easily swing your arms and legs.

2. HINGE: This joint opens and closes like a door. It lets you bend and extend your elbows and knees.

3. PIVOT: One of these joints is found at the top of your spine. It allows for rotation, so that you can turn your head from side to side.

4. GLIDING: This joint is located between two flat bones that glide against each other, such as those in your wrists and ankles. It mainly allows for sideways movement.

Living Lost

Have you ever been lost? If so, it probably happened when you were in unfamiliar surroundings. But people with developmental topographical disorientation (DTD) regularly get lost in familiar places, like their own neighborhoods or even their own homes! The first case of DTD was discovered by neuroscientist Dr. Giuseppe Iaria of the University of Calgary in 2009. Another 120 cases were confirmed by the end of the following year. And people continue to be diagnosed with DTD each day.

MAP IT OUT

According to Dr. Iaria, one of the major problems for people with DTD is that they are unable to form "cognitive maps." These are sort of like everyday road maps, except they exist in the brain. As we become familiar with a new place, we notice the landmarks around us, like buildings, signs, and trees. We note their locations and where they are in relation to each other. This creates a cognitive map that helps us picture in our mind where

things are. Since those with DTD never develop the ability to form cognitive maps, they get lost even in places that are part of their daily lives.

STARTING YOUNG

Imagine how challenging life would be if you got lost at every turn. Unfortunately, treating people with DTD can be nearly impossible once they reach adulthood. That's why Dr. Iaria has begun to focus his studies on children with DTD. If these kids can be trained to form cognitive maps early in life, it may give them a chance to overcome the condition. Dr. Iaria is developing a special video game that will identify if a child has DTD and then train her to form mental maps in her head.

Sharon Roseman of Littleton, Colorado, shares her experience of living with DTD.

Have you always had DTD?

The earliest memory of my having DTD was when I was five years old. I was playing blind man's bluff with my friends out in front of my house. When the blindfold was removed from my eyes, I had no idea where I was. Nothing I could see was familiar to me.

When did you first realize it was an actual condition?

I didn't know until about five years ago, at the age of about sixty-one, when I was put in touch with Dr. Iaria, who was doing research on DTD. It was a huge relief to know that I wasn't the only person who experienced this.

IMPROVE YOUR INNER GPS

- Figure out where north, south, east, and west are when you are in different places.

- Learn to read a map and try locating landmarks on it.

- Play games or puzzles that test your sense of space, like tangrams, jigsaw puzzles, and mazes.

- Pay attention to how long it takes you to walk or bike from point A to point B. This will help you improve your sense of distance and your navigation skills.

Can you explain what it feels like to have DTD?

Nothing looks right. Each time I am presented with a curve in a road or an angled pathway, my brain will suddenly see things turned the wrong way again. This can happen many, many times each day. There are many other scenarios that can cause DTD to happen for me: sleeping, being in a lake or a swimming pool, driving in the mountains, being in a large park or at a zoo or a mall, where there are many areas going in many different directions.

Do you actually become lost in a familiar setting, like your own home?

Yes, I can get lost in my own home or in any familiar setting.

How does the condition affect your daily life?

I try to have a good attitude about things when I continually get lost, but it's not always easy. Since I now know and understand why these things happen to me, I am more comfortable telling people about it, and they are more than willing to help me any way they can.

Have you developed any strategies to cope with your DTD?

My coping strategies involve constantly routing my day on streets that are perfectly straight...no curves, no angles. It may take me double or triple the amount of time to get to where I need to be, but I'm willing to do that so I can avoid as many obstacles as possible that can trigger a DTD episode.

That's Not Music to My Ears

AMUSIA
(ay-MYOO-zee-uh)

It's hard to imagine someone getting no pleasure from listening to music. After all, music can lift your spirits, take you back to a great memory, and get you singing at the top of your lungs. But for those with amusia, music is completely unenjoyable. In some instances, amusics—people who have this condition—actually find it painful to listen to music. The brain of an amusic can't detect a difference between notes, so every song sounds like a rattling, banging mess. About 4 percent of people have amusia. For them, one song sounds like the next. So "Happy Birthday to You" is no different from the latest tune topping the charts—and both are an annoyance.

IT'S A MATTER OF MATTER

Most amusics are born with the condition, and it's thought to run in families. A recent study by amusia expert Dr. Isabelle Peretz and her colleagues at the Université de Montréal found that amusics have less white matter in the front area of the brain than others. This reduces the communication between the front of the brain and a region called the auditory cortex. It's here where sounds, like music, are interpreted. This lack of communication makes it difficult for an amusic's brain to recognize music as anything but noise.

Studies have shown that 90 percent of us get an "earworm" at least once a week.

No need to panic, though. An earworm is just a song that gets stuck in your head for minutes, hours, or even days at a time. Researchers at the Université de Montréal discovered that some songs are "stickier" than others. Tunes that have repetitive lyrics or phrases will undoubtedly set off the "repeat" button in your head. And a 2011 British study found that an earworm often occurs when your mind is wandering or you're doing something that doesn't require much thought, such as walking.

WHY MUSIC MATTERS

You might think that you could live without music in your life. But consider how important music is to us and how often we pop on headphones to get our daily fix. We connect to certain tunes—some can even make us feel better when our day isn't going well. Music is important in our social worlds, too. It brings people together in a way few things can. Imagine a party without some tunes being cranked. For many amusics, an event like a get-together or a concert is something that they dread because they're forced to endure the constant melodies and rhythms that fill the air. Music is not enjoyable, creative, or even inspiring to them—it's just irritating.

LET'S DANCE... OR MAYBE NOT

Another condition, known as beat deafness, gives a whole new meaning to having two left feet. It was first documented in 2011, when researchers at the Université de Montréal discovered a person, identified only as Mathieu, who couldn't detect the beat in music. Though he could recognize different tones and was able to sing in tune, Mathieu was hopeless when it came to finding the beat and dancing to it. Like amusia, beat deafness is thought to be an issue with flawed connections within the brain.

The Tale of the Tongue

Scientists have discovered that we experience taste in completely different ways. About 25 percent of people are born with a heightened sense of taste. They're called supertasters, and they are extremely sensitive to the flavors of food. Taste researcher Dr. Linda Bartoshuk discovered the existence of these superpowered tasters about twenty years ago. She determined that people can be split into three groups: supertasters, normal tasters, and non-tasters. Most people—about 50 percent—fall into the normal tasters category, while 25 percent are non-tasters. They can taste, just not as well.

AN ABUNDANCE OF BUDS

According to Dr. Bartoshuk, a supertaster's ability comes down to the number of taste buds that are found on the tongue. Taste buds are clusters of nerve endings that allow us to experience different flavors. Dr. Bartoshuk found that supertasters are born with an unusually high number of buds, which causes them to have a superior sense of taste. Some scientists suggest that having a sense of supertaste may trace back to our ancestors. In the past, taste was key to survival, because it helped people quickly recognize the bitter flavor of unsafe or toxic plants.

FOOD FOR THOUGHT

Being a supertaster can have an impact on a person's diet. All those extra taste buds make flavors more potent, so supertasters find certain foods unenjoyable to eat. Items on the bottom of their list include spicy foods and strong-flavored, bitter foods, like broccoli and grapefruit. Researchers have also found that supertasters shy away from fatty and sweet foods, such as rich chocolate cake. This may explain why supertasters tend to be thinner than those with a typical sense of taste. However, these taste champs don't have perfect eating habits. Supertasters often eat fewer fruits and veggies because they dislike their flavors.

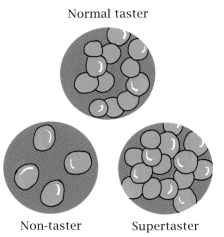

Normal taster

Non-taster   Supertaster

FAST FACT
Taste buds are replaced every two weeks.

Dr. Virginia Utermohlen of New York State shares her experiences of living as a supertaster.

THE TASTE-SMELL COMBO

You've probably noticed that you can't taste very well when your nose is stuffed up. That's because your senses of taste and smell work together to give you a complete picture of what you're eating. While your taste buds are doing their thing, odors float up through the back of your mouth to receptors in your nose. Those receptors signal to the brain that there's an incoming aroma. Your brain combines the taste and smell messages to determine what flavor you're munching on.

When did you first realize that you were a supertaster?

I have always known—ever since I was very little—that I taste things that other people don't. For example, I remember the rubbery taste that my mother's spatula transferred to whipped cream.

How does the condition affect your everyday life?

I have always been a very particular eater. There are certain flavors that I have never liked, and certain flavors that I adore to excess. For the flavors I don't like, even a trace can make an otherwise delicious meal taste foul. And I can't get enough of the flavors that I like, so I often go overboard.

Are there any disadvantages to being a supertaster?

Definitely. It limits what you can choose to eat at a restaurant. Often there may be only one or two things that I can be sure I will like on a menu. It also makes for trouble when I go for a meal at another person's home. People get insulted when I catalogue all the foods I don't like.

Do you think there are advantages to being a supertaster?

There are a couple. First, I can be completely absorbed in eating something truly delicious, which is a wonderful feeling. Second, there is the ability to know right away when something has spoiled.

Are there particular foods or flavors that you avoid because of your taste sensitivity?

A big long list, in fact, including corn, fresh tomatoes, Brussels sprouts, green beans, carrots…most nuts, yogurt, milk chocolate, hot chili peppers, and many more. Plus, there are foods I have never tasted because I thought I might not like them and I didn't want to subject myself to unpleasantness.

That Sound in Your Head

In spite of its name, exploding head syndrome (EHS) doesn't result in an exploding head! Also known as sensory sleep starts, EHS happens when a person is first drifting off to sleep. Out of the blue, a loud bang is heard inside her head. The sound has been compared to a clash of cymbals or a slamming of doors. This noise startles the person awake, and it's common for her to see bright lights for a moment. Once she's awake, the sound disappears. Sleep neurologist Dr. Kirstie Anderson says EHS isn't a serious problem. Many of us are woken up by an occasional jerk of the body as we drift off—those with EHS just hear a noise instead.

WHAT'S GOING ON IN THERE?

Dr. Anderson suggests that since EHS usually happens as someone is dozing off, the condition is probably triggered by the brain moving too quickly from wakefulness into deeper sleep. It's unclear why some people hear an explosive sound during this transition. Sometimes attacks of exploding head syndrome may happen in clusters over several nights, but then they may disappear for months or even years at a time—or even forever.

I JUST WANT SOME SHUT-EYE

While it may not have any harmful physical effects, exploding head syndrome can cause worry for sufferers. The fear of experiencing another episode of EHS can make people nervous about going to sleep and occasionally leads to insomnia, a condition where people find it difficult to fall asleep. There isn't any treatment for EHS, but Dr. Anderson suggests that if a patient is reassured she is in no danger, this often helps to calm fears.

WHY DO WE SLEEP?

Without sleep, we feel sluggish and grumpy, and we often have a hard time performing tasks. If we avoid sleep for a few nights, we may start to hallucinate, or see things that aren't really there. That said, scientists are still curious about why we spend one-third of our lives snoozing. Here are some theories:

- We need sleep for our **IMMUNE SYSTEMS** to work well.

- Rest gives our bodies **TIME TO RESTORE AND REPAIR** cells, muscles, and other body tissues.

- Sleep is important for **MEMORY AND LEARNING**—it allows our brains to sort and store information collected during the day.

- We **SAVE ENERGY** when we sleep. This was especially useful for our ancestors, who had less access to food, and therefore fewer sources of body energy.

THAT'S THE SOUND OF YOUR EYEBALLS

For a person with something called superior canal dehiscence syndrome (SCDS), it's not uncommon to hear strange sounds coming from inside his head. This disorder causes noises within the body to be magnified. So a person may hear his own heart beating, his joints moving, or even the sound of his eyeballs moving in their sockets! The condition occurs because part of a bone near the inner ear is missing, so sounds are amplified in the affected ear. Luckily, surgery can repair the problem.

FAST FACT

Women experience exploding head syndrome more often than men. And people over the age of fifty are more likely to have the condition.

The World in Technicolor

The average human can see about one million different colors. But Dr. Gabriele Jordan, a neuroscientist at Newcastle University in England, recently discovered a woman who can see about one hundred million colors. The British woman, identified only as Mrs. M, is the first person known to have supercolor vision, or tetrachromacy. Mrs. M can detect subtle shades of colors that are invisible to the rest of us, which is the reason for her superior vision. Dr. Jordan estimates that 2 to 3 percent of women probably have this super-special condition but have yet to be identified. (Men can't have tetrachromacy because of their genetics.)

SOMETHING EXTRA

Mrs. M and other tetrachromats have such incredible color vision because of the number of cone receptors they have. Cone receptors are specialized cells in the eye's retina. Each receptor can pick up one of three colors—red, blue, or green. A typical person has three cone receptors in each eye. Since the brain can combine different shades of red, blue, and green, we can see about one million colors with those three receptors. A tetrachromat has one additional cone receptor between the red and green receptors. It picks up shades of orange, and it's this fourth cone that allows someone like Mrs. M to see significantly more colors.

HOW COME?

One thing that puzzles Dr. Jordan and other tetrachromacy researchers is why some women have four cone receptors but are not tetrachromats. They can see only the same colors as the rest of us. Why this happens is a mystery.

THE SCIENCE OF COLOR

We see in color thanks to a tag-team effort by our eyes and brain. All the colors of the spectrum are found in light. When we look at something, like a red flower, the spectrum of colors is shining on it. The flower absorbs all the colored light rays except red. This red light is reflected off the flower and travels to our eyes. It enters the cornea, pupil, and lens and reaches cells at the back of the eye called photoreceptors. These receptors turn the light into electrical impulses that then travel along the optic nerve to the brain, which gets a message that the flower is red.

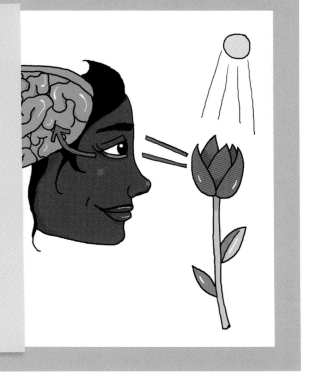

WHY ARE SOME PEOPLE COLOR BLIND?

People who are color blind can usually still see in color, but they have difficulty telling certain hues apart. The most common type of color blindness is red–green, in which a person has trouble distinguishing between some shades of red and green. The rarest form is called monochromatism, and it's when every color appears to be a shade of gray. Color blindness is caused by a defect in the cone receptors. If a receptor doesn't work properly, a person will struggle to distinguish between some colors. That said, there are people with color blindness who can actually identify several specific colors better than those with so-called normal color vision.

TESTING!

Look at these images. They're often used to determine if someone has color blindness. What numbers do you see inside the circles? Those who can clearly see the number within each pattern of dots (left: 4, right: 8) generally have normal color vision. Those who find it difficult may be color blind.

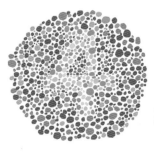

Down the Rabbit Hole

For someone with Alice in Wonderland Syndrome (AIWS), the world can suddenly look like a funhouse come to life. Objects temporarily appear smaller or larger than they really are. For instance, a person's hand may seem to stretch across the room. A friend may look to be the size of an action figure. Or a doorknob may appear to be the same size as the door itself. These wonky images have nothing to do with the person's eyes. It's simply how the brain is "seeing" things at that moment. An episode typically lasts anywhere from a few seconds to fifteen minutes. After that, everything looks normal again. AIWS occurs mainly in kids, and most have symptoms right as a headache begins or before they drift off to sleep. As for the condition's name, it comes from the main character in Lewis Carroll's book *Alice's Adventures in Wonderland*. Carroll is thought to have suffered from AIWS, and it's believed this inspired the book's fantastical world.

IT DOESN'T STOP THERE

AIWS can also affect other senses. There are times when a person may feel as if sounds are getting louder when they're not. Or he may feel like his feet are sinking into the floor as he walks along. In other instances, time gets distorted—a moment seems to speed up or slow down. All these warped experiences may be troubling, but experts say AIWS isn't dangerous and rarely becomes a problem in a person's daily life.

MAKING SENSE OF IT

Scientists believe this syndrome involves a few areas of the brain, including the occipital lobe, which manages your vision. Once this region processes what you see, the information is sent to the temporal lobe. As this data moves along, your brain is figuring out the location and size of the objects you're looking at. Neurologist Dr. William Young suggests that in those with AIWS, a glitch occurs as the information passes between the two lobes, leading to objects being seen in a distorted way.

BLAME THAT ACHE IN YOUR HEAD

Research shows that AIWS affects people who suffer from migraine headaches or have a family history of headaches. Some experts refer to an attack of AIWS as a mini-migraine exploding in the brain. Dr. Young thinks that these episodes could be caused by migraines occurring near the brain's occipital and temporal lobes. While there's currently no cure for the syndrome, most kids will outgrow it in their teens.

A PAIN IN THE HEAD

Each day, millions of people suffer from headaches. While it may seem as if it's your brain that hurts, the ache is actually around the brain. Pain is felt by nerve endings and blood vessels within your skull. There are several types of headaches:

- **Tension headaches:** These are the most frequent kind—they're usually felt as a dull, steady pain across the forehead or on both sides of the head at the temples. Eyestrain or tightness in your shoulders, neck, or jaw muscles may cause these headaches.

- **Migraines:** These headaches are often felt as a throbbing pain on one side of the head. They can have other symptoms, including nausea and a sensitivity to light or noise. Stress, weather changes, a lack of sleep, and too much caffeine can all trigger a migraine.

- **Secondary headaches:** These are the headaches that come about as a result of being sick with a virus, like the flu. Once the illness disappears, so does the headache.

I SCREAM, YOU SCREAM, WE ALL SCREAM BECAUSE OF ICE CREAM

Anyone who has gobbled up ice cream too quickly has probably had brain freeze. This ache happens when the roof of your mouth senses the cold treat, causing its blood vessels to expand quickly. Nerves in your mouth think these swelling vessels mean you're in pain. They send a pain message to your brain, and you get a headache. To stop brain freeze, simply put your tongue on the roof of your mouth. Its warmth will calm the nerves and end that ache.

HANDS-ON RESEARCH

While a person with AIWS may have moments when he thinks parts of his body look distorted, a 2010 study found that most of us generally have a warped view of our hands. Scientists at University College London determined that people tend to think their hands are shorter and wider than they really are. The researchers had eighteen volunteers place their left hands on a table, and then they covered them. When the volunteers were asked to describe the size of their hands, 80 percent judged them as being wider. And the majority believed their fingers were shorter than their actual size. The researchers say our brain is the reason for this distorted view—they believe the confusion has to do with how the brain gathers information from different areas of the body.

Place That Face

Most people have had the experience of not remembering someone they've already met. But those with face blindness, or prosopagnosia, never recognize a face. It's as if everyone is a stranger. They can't place faces that they've seen countless times, including those of family members and friends. In some cases, they don't even recognize themselves in a mirror! It isn't a question of being unable to see properly. Those with face blindness can see facial features. They just can't piece them together to see a face as a whole. Some individuals develop face blindness after a brain injury, but many are born with the condition.

FACING THE FACTS

Face blindness was first identified in the 1940s, but experts still aren't sure what causes it. Dr. Bradley Duchaine, a brain sciences professor who has spent over fifteen years studying the condition, says that research has unlocked some clues. Those who struggle to recognize faces appear to have problems in two regions found at the back of the brain—the temporal and occipital lobes. These spots respond strongly to faces rather than objects like houses or cars. Dr. Duchaine explains that brain responses in these areas are weaker for those with face blindness, which is probably why they can't place a face.

GETTING BY

Those who live with face blindness don't always realize they have the condition. They often assume that they're just not very good at remembering faces. Many reach adulthood before they realize they have an issue that others don't have to deal with. To cope with it, face-blind individuals learn to pay attention to other features. They may zero in on a voice, hairstyle, or piece of clothing to figure out who a person is.

FAST FACT

Some people have a condition that's the opposite of face blindness. Super recognizers never forget a face they've seen.

WHAT'S IT LIKE?

Andrea Ray of Kansas shares her experience of living with face blindness.

When did you first realize that you were face blind?

I remember not knowing who people were when I was five years old. But I didn't read about face blindness until I was forty-five and read about other people's experiences. After saying, "Hey, that happens to me a lot!" I realized I might be face blind.

How would you explain what it feels like to be face blind?

I cannot picture the faces of the people I love, not even those of my children. It's frustrating when someone doesn't believe me or understand my explanations.

They wave their hand and dismiss it, saying, "Oh, I have trouble knowing who people are, and I can't remember names." But that's different. They can recognize faces. They get an "I know you" feeling. But I rarely get that feeling.

Can you explain what you see when you look at someone's face?

I can see all the parts: brows, eyes, nose, ears, mouth, and chin. I know how those parts go together, and I can tell people's expressions. But what my brain does not do is put the parts together to make the whole face that's always the same person. Photos of someone from different angles are like different people to me. If I glimpse my reflection in a mirror, I don't recognize myself, but I know it must be me.

How does the condition affect your daily life?

I get left out of conversations about popular shows and movies. I don't watch many because I can't keep track of the characters. Sports and war movies are the worst because uniforms make everyone identical. I can't find my family in a crowd because their faces don't "pop out." In grade school, I didn't know most of my classmates or realize that many were the same from year to year.

Do you have any strategies that you use to identify people?

I work on memorizing unusual features—hairstyles, mustaches and beards, body shapes, clothes, the way someone walks, voices—and then adding their name to these features.

My, What a Lot of Teeth You Have!

Humans are normally born with twenty primary (or baby) teeth and some of their thirty-two permanent ones. The teeth aren't visible at birth, but they develop under the gums and in the jawbone while a baby is in its mother's belly. However, those with supernumerary teeth, or hyperdontia, are born with extra teeth. Sometimes this means an entire extra set! These supernumerary teeth can be found in any region of the mouth, but the most common is an almost shark-like tooth poking through the gums between the two upper front incisors. In other cases, a person may have extra molars, and some people end up with hard lumps of dental tissue that don't resemble a tooth at all.

THEY'RE OUTTA THERE

Dentists estimate that about 1 percent of the population has supernumerary teeth. These extra teeth may cause crowding or prevent the permanent ones from erupting through the gums altogether. And this can lead right to a dentist's chair. Supernumerary teeth often have to be pulled to prevent these kinds of dental issues.

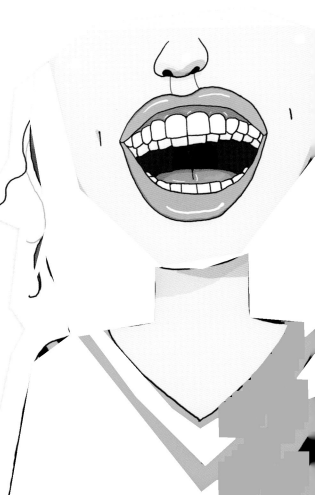

THE TOOTH TRUTH

Hyperdontia seems to be a hereditary condition, or a trait you inherit from your parents. There are a couple of theories about why people end up with bonus teeth. Some experts believe that the tooth bud—a mass of tissue that eventually forms a tooth—inexplicably divides and causes two separate teeth to form. Another guess is that the region of cells where teeth form—called the dental lamina—somehow becomes overactive, leading to the development of extra teeth.

You have four kinds of teeth in that mouth of yours.

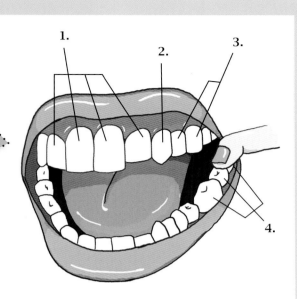

HERE TO STAY

Baby teeth usually start to appear around six months of age, and most permanent teeth are in place by around age twelve. But for those with a condition called hypodontia, permanent teeth don't develop at all. These individuals often have to live with several baby teeth into adulthood. In some cases, the baby teeth have to be removed and replaced with artificial teeth because they just aren't strong enough to get the job done.

1. **INCISORS (or cutting teeth):** The eight teeth found in the front of your mouth have a straight, sharp edge for cutting and biting food.

2. **CANINES:** These four teeth are the strong ones located beside your incisors. They are pointed to make it easy to hold and tear food.

3. **BICUSPIDS (or premolars):** These eight flat teeth are used for chewing. They're located behind the canines.

4. **MOLARS:** You have twelve molars in the back of your mouth. These teeth have a wide, flat surface—they're used for the final chewing and grinding of food before you swallow it. The third molars—the ones at the very back of our mouths—are also known as wisdom teeth.

FAST FACT

Your teeth are covered in enamel. It's the strongest substance in your body.

It's Hair-Raising

Uncombable hair syndrome (UHS) may sound like another way to describe a bad hair day, but it's a genuine problem. The condition usually appears between the ages of three months and twelve years. Unlike normal hair, which bends as you run your fingers through it, this hair sticks out straight and won't bend a bit. This makes it impossible to comb flat. UHS is sometimes called "doll hair," because the hair is as unruly as a doll's can become over time. UHS was first described in 1973, and since then fewer than one hundred cases have been reported. Those with UHS usually have light blond locks, and their hair is dry, curly, and breaks easily.

HAIR'S THE FACTS

In 1985, dermatologist Dr. Walter Shelley examined hair from patients with UHS. After looking at the strands under a microscope, he discovered they had unusual grooves running along the length of them. Dr. Shelley also found that the strands had a triangular shape, whereas normal hair strands are oval. He determined that these are possible reasons for the hair's unruly appearance.

HANG IN THERE

UHS runs in families, but researchers have not yet identified the gene that causes the hairy issue. It's not all bad news for UHS sufferers, though. While it may be frustrating to have hair that stands at attention day and night, experts have found that UHS generally improves once a child hits his teen years. At that point, the hair usually—and mysteriously—begins to grow in normally.

Get a close-up look at the way a strand of hair develops.

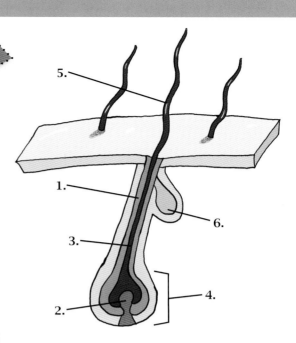

WHAT'S WITH ALL THIS HAIR?

Your body is covered in hair—although some of it is hard to see, since it's so fine and short. (Imagine if it weren't!) In fact, the palms of your hands and the soles of your feet are about the only places you won't find hair. Hair serves a number of purposes:

- That mop on your head protects you from the harmful rays of the sun, and it also keeps you from losing too much body heat through your head.

- Eyebrows prevent sweat from dripping into your eyes and affecting your vision.

- Eyelashes catch dirt and other particles before they can enter and irritate your eyes.

- Nose hairs trap dirt and bacteria until you blow or sneeze them away.

- Those tiny hairs on other parts of your body, such as your arms and legs, are leftover from your furry ancestors, who needed body hair to keep warm.

1. **FOLLICLE:** The structure where a hair grows.

2. **DERMAL PAPILLA:** A small projection containing tiny blood vessels that feed hair cells.

3. **ROOT:** The base of a hair.

4. **BULB:** Found at the bottom of a hair root, the bulb produces hair cells, or keratin. As new cells form, they push up on the old ones—this creates a strand of hair.

5. **HAIR SHAFT:** The hair itself. A single hair on the head grows for two to six years. Then it falls out and the follicle rests for a few months.

6. **SEBACEOUS GLAND:** An oil gland that's attached to each hair. It keeps the strands shiny.

FACT: Once a strand of hair is at the skin's surface, it contains only dead cells. That's why it doesn't hurt when you get a haircut.

FAST FACT

Uncombable hair syndrome only affects the hair on the head.

Making Sense of It

Most people think of their five senses—sight, hearing, taste, smell, and touch—separately. But those with synesthesia experience two senses at the same time. That's because one triggers a reaction from another. For example, a person who has synesthesia may taste chocolate every time she hears a specific song. So the sound she's hearing is also perceived by her sense of taste. In rare forms of the condition, a synesthete (that's a person who has synesthesia) may smell a specific scent when she sees a certain object or even hear a particular sound when she touches an item. These reactions are completely automatic and involuntary.

DOUBLE DUTY

Synesthesia can involve any two of the five senses. But the way those two senses are experienced is almost always unique to the person. So while one person may hear a bell and taste peaches, another will taste licorice when he hears the same sound. Experts suggest that one in every 200 people probably has some form of synesthesia. And the condition is said to be harmless.

"B" IS BLUE

In the most common form of synesthesia, a person joins objects such as numbers or letters of the alphabet with distinct colors. A synesthete might see the letter M as bright yellow, for example, or the number 2 as navy blue. Each letter or number is usually the same color whenever she sees it. And it will stay the same throughout her lifetime. The color does, however, differ from person to person.

THE REASON WHY

Though synesthesia is still a mystery, Dr. Vilayanur Ramachandran, a neuroscientist at the University of California, San Diego, thinks it may be caused by an accidental cross-wiring in the brain. We know the two areas of the brain responsible for helping us process numbers and colors lie directly beside each other. Dr. Ramachandran theorizes that when a synesthete sees a number, communication occurs between both these areas of the brain. So the number is seen as a color. Another synesthesia expert, Dr. Veronica Gross, says there is evidence to support this cross-wired theory. Studies of synesthetes have found that some of these individuals do have extra connections between certain areas of their brains.

TASTES LIKE MUSIC

Musical synesthesia is a rare form of the condition in which people taste music. That means every time a synesthete hears a song, her sense of taste kicks in, too. Particular notes in a song could have a salty flavor. Others may have a sweetness to them. And still other notes might have the taste and texture of a particular food, like celery or pineapple. As with other forms of synesthesia, the tastes differ for each person. There are also other instances when a synesthete will listen to a song and see shapes or colors for the different notes, tones, and harmonies of the tune.

Alison Buckholtz of Washington, DC, shares her experience of having synesthesia.

SOUNDS LIKE YELLOW

In 2013, researchers from the University of California, Berkeley, found that people's brains are naturally wired to connect music with color. Participants in their study were asked to pick the color that they felt matched several pieces of classical music. Time and again, they associated bright colors—like yellows and oranges—with upbeat and fast-paced songs. And they matched slower-paced, sad melodies with dull grays and blues.

FAST FACT

"Synesthesia" comes from the Greek words *syn* (together) and *aesthesia* (sensation).

When did you first realize that you had synesthesia?

For much of my childhood, I didn't even realize that experiencing two senses at once was unusual because it was normal for me. Later, as I became a teenager and became more self-conscious, wanting to fit in and be like everyone else, I came to understand that no one else seemed to experience the world the same way I did. I knew that if others heard me talk about seeing numbers as colors or people as colors, they would think I was weird. When I was in my late twenties, I heard a report about synesthesia, and that was the first time I ever connected it with me.

How would you explain what it feels like to have synesthesia?

It feels completely normal, because it's normal for the person who experiences it. Looking back, I see that it sparked my imagination and creativity in many ways.

Does the condition ever get in the way of your everyday life?

I think that seeing numbers as colors both helped and hindered me in math. Sometimes it helped me remember things because I associated each number with a color; sometimes it was very overwhelming and gave me a headache.

Do you think there are advantages to having synesthesia?

There are definitely advantages. It has allowed me to see the world around me in a different way from everyone else, and to be able to experience and describe something in an original way is a gift. I hated this feeling of being "different" as a child, but as an adult, knowing that I can contribute a new perspective on something makes me more confident.

I Saw the Light... and Sneezed

A sneeze is a reflex. That means you don't think about it; it just happens. And it's unstoppable. Sneezing is the body's way of ridding the nose of germs, dust, and irritants so they don't end up in your lungs. But for one-third of the population, a sneeze lets loose for another reason: those with photic sneeze reflex can't help sneezing when exposed to bright light. When a photic sneezer enters daylight after leaving a dark place, like a movie theater or a tunnel, an uncontrollable sneezing spree begins. It's usually a burst of one to ten sneezes. In rare cases, people sneeze up to fifty times in a row. Sun sneezing—as it's also called—is an inherited condition.

MENTAL MIX-UP

Scientists think that photic sneezing is caused by a mix-up between two nerves that are very close to each other in the brain. The trigeminal nerve lets us know when we need to sneeze and the optic nerve tells us what our eyes are seeing. When we see a bright light, the optic nerve sends an electrical signal to the brain telling it to reduce the size of our pupils (this controls how much light can enter the eye). It's thought that when a sun sneezer sees a bright light, the trigeminal nerve receives this signal, too. It's mistaken by the brain as a need to sneeze, so the "achooing" begins.

WHY CAN'T WE SNEEZE WITH OUR EYES OPEN?

Closing our eyes is an automatic response. They shut tight after receiving a signal from the brain that a sneeze is on the way. But the idea that sneezing with your eyes open will cause them to pop out of their sockets is pure fiction. If you manage to keep them open, the muscles that are attached to your eyeballs will hold them firmly in place.

Get in the know (or nose!) with these facts about sneezing.

NAME: The scientific term for a sneeze is sternutation.

SPEED OF A SNEEZE: The average sneeze leaves your nose at up to 100 mph (160 km/h).

NUMBER OF PARTICLES: One sneeze can produce 2,500 to 5,000 droplets of saliva and mucus.

SNEEZY SPRAY: Those droplets can fly 5 ft. (1.5 m) from the nostrils.

LONGEST SNEEZE SPREE: A British girl sneezed at least once every five minutes for 978 days.

SNEEZIEST ANIMAL: Iguanas sneeze more than any other creature.

ANATOMY OF A SNEEZE

1. **CILIA**—the tiny hair-like structures found in the lining of the nose—trap many of the irritating particles that enter the nostrils.

2. **NERVE ENDINGS**, or receptors, in the upper lining of the nose detect an irritation in the nasal passages. They send a message to the "sneeze center," which is found in an area of the lower brain stem called the medulla.

3. The brain signals **FACIAL NERVES** and **MUSCLES** in the abdomen, chest, and throat to prepare for a sneeze.

4. The brain tells the **EYES** and **MOUTH** to close.

5. **CONTRACTING MUSCLES** in the chest and throat push out air, which creates the sneeze. Thousands of tiny bacteria-filled particles explode from the nose and mouth.

FAST FACT

Some scientists refer to photic sneeze syndrome as autosomal dominant compelling helio-ophthalmic outburst syndrome. That's ACHOO, for short!

Print-Free People

It's a part of you that often gets left behind when you leave a room—fingerprints. These patterned ridges develop while you're a baby growing inside your mom. And they don't change during your lifetime. But scientists recently came across four families whose members don't have any fingerprints at all. They appear to be the only people on the planet with a fingerprint-free condition called adermatoglyphia. These individuals also lack prints on the palms of their hands and soles of their feet.

ALL IN THE FAMILY

In 2011, dermatologist Dr. Eli Sprecher studied the DNA (a molecule found in your cells that tells your body how to develop) of sixteen members of a family from Switzerland. Seven members of this large family have fingerprints, while nine don't have a print in sight. Dr. Sprecher and researchers in Switzerland and Israel discovered that the members with no fingerprints had a mutated, or altered, gene. This gene affects fingerprint development while a baby is forming. Now that scientists have put their finger on this information, they're investigating how fingerprint patterns form, which is still a mystery.

WHY DO WE HAVE FINGERPRINTS?

Here are some theories about the function of these grooved ridges:

- It's commonly believed that fingerprints help improve our grip on objects. But in 2009, researchers at the University of Manchester, in England, conducted experiments that proved fingerprints actually reduce our grip on smooth objects. They may, however, help us hold on to rough items.

- The same researchers theorized that fingerprints allow water to drain away from our fingertips, giving us a better grasp on objects in wet conditions.

- Some experts have found that fingerprints improve our sense of touch. The ridges appear to help nerve endings sense textures better than smooth fingertips would.

FAST FACT

Like fingerprints, tongue prints are unique to each individual on Earth.

HOW GROOVY

Everyone has unique fingerprints— even identical twins. There are three main types of ridge patterns.

1. **WHORL:** This pattern features ridges that are circular.

2. **LOOP:** The ridges begin on one side of the finger, curve around, and go back the same way. This is the most common type of human fingerprint.

3. **ARCH:** The ridges flow from one side of the finger to the other with a slight rise in the middle. This is the least common type of print.

People Power

Now and then we hear stories of ordinary people performing extraordinary feats of strength. A mother lifts a car off her child. A man fights off a bear that's attacking him. Or a firefighter rips off a car door to save a trapped passenger. According to experts, when we're under intense pressure, most of us are capable of super strength. In a stressful situation, our nervous system—the body's main control center—takes over. Our heart starts pumping faster, which sends more blood and oxygen to our muscles. This gives them an extra boost that can provide us with unusual strength, at least for a short while.

THE FEAR FACTOR

Fear plays an important role in super strength. When we're faced with danger, a region of the brain called the hypothalamus starts working overtime. It's part of the nervous system, and it translates information from the brain to control functions like body temperature, hunger, and thirst. The hypothalamus tells the body to release a chemical called adrenaline into the bloodstream. This rush of adrenaline is what makes the heart and lungs speed up, which in turn prepares the muscles for action. Vision even narrows to allow us to focus on the task at hand. All of this helps us perform feats of strength we'd normally find impossible.

GO WITH THE FLOW

Experts believe that endorphins—hormones released in the brain—also help people muster up super strength. Endorphins work with cells in the brain to temporarily block out pain during stressful or risky situations. If you don't feel pain, then you don't feel your muscles straining. And this allows you to take advantage of the temporary increase in your power. Of course, there can be consequences that come with pushing yourself too far.

While you may not feel pain during a bout of super strength, your body will often experience the effects later in the form of muscle or joint damage.

MADE OF MUSCLES

Your body is packed with over 600 muscles. They work hard to help you do anything that requires motion—climbing a tree, throwing a ball, smiling, even digesting your food. There are three types of muscles:

- **SKELETAL:** These are the muscles that you move and control, such as those in your arms and legs.

- **SMOOTH:** Found throughout your body, these muscles work without your having to think about it. Your stomach and intestines are examples.

- **CARDIAC:** These thick muscles are found in one place—the wall of your heart.

DELTOIDS: These muscles allow for movement in your shoulders. They help you do things like throw and shrug.

BICEPS: You see your biceps when you flex your arms. These muscles allow you to bend at the elbow and are used when you throw an object or brush your teeth.

ABDOMINALS: Also called abs, these muscles support your body and are used when you walk or run. You'll feel them tense up when you laugh hard—or bust a gut.

PECTORALS: These chest muscles are used when you lift your arms and move your shoulders forward. They are also needed when doing push-ups.

QUADRICEPS: These leg muscles are used often during the day. You rely on your quadriceps to straighten the leg at the knee. They help you stand up from a sitting position.

GLUTEUS MAXIMUS: Found in your bottom, this largest muscle in the body helps you climb stairs, stand up, and of course, sit down.

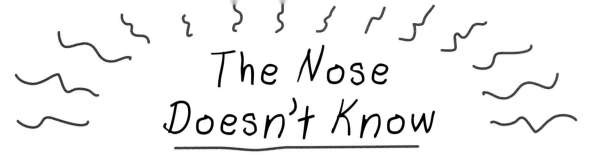

The Nose Doesn't Know

Most humans can detect more than 10,000 different smells. But about 1 percent of people have no sense of smell at all. Those with isolated congenital anosmia cannot detect any scent from the time they are born throughout their entire lifetime. The rare condition is believed to be inherited, and it has no other symptoms. Many anosmic young kids don't even realize they can't smell until they get older and begin to understand that others have that ability.

THE SMELL SYSTEM

Experts have long believed that the olfactory system—the region responsible for detecting odors—fails to develop properly in those with congenital anosmia. Normally, scent particles enter our nostrils and attach to a layer of tissue called the olfactory epithelium. In this tissue there are about 25 million receptor cells, each of which is covered in cilia. When an odor attaches to the cilia, the receptors send electrical signals to the brain so the scent can be identified. If there's a problem with the olfactory system, some people may not be able to smell.

REGROWN SENSE

True anosmics are born with the condition, but others lose their sense of smell after a head injury. Amazingly, these individuals can sometimes regain their lost sense. That's because, unlike most brain cells, the cells that control your sense of smell have an ability to regrow.

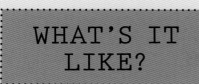

WHAT'S IT LIKE?

This is your author speaking! It's true. I, Maria Birmingham, have congenital anosmia. I haven't been able to smell a thing since day one on the planet.

SMELLS LIKE A MEMORY

Have you ever caught a whiff of a particular smell and had a memory come rushing back? The link occurs in the brain's limbic system, also known as the emotional brain. Here you'll find the olfactory bulb (which receives smell signals from the nose) as well as two areas involved in memory, the amygdala and the hippocampus. When you smell something, your brain stores the emotion that came with it in these two areas. The next time you smell this scent, the amygdala and hippocampus instantly call up the memory linked with it.

FAST FACT

When we reach our sixties, many humans begin to experience a reduced sense of smell.

When did I first know I couldn't smell?

I have no memory of when I first realized I had no sense of smell. My parents noticed I couldn't smell when I was about two or three and didn't react to a particularly strong odor in the room. They took me to the doctor and found I was otherwise perfectly healthy.

Does my condition affect my sense of taste?

The number one question I always get is: Can you taste? And the answer is: yes. I suppose people find it surprising, since taste and smell are so closely linked. But I can taste everything from salty snacks (my fave!) to sour lemons. I'm guessing my sense of taste isn't as fine-tuned as yours, though. When I'm eating candy, I can't tell the difference between flavors—they all just taste sweet to me.

Do I feel like I'm missing out?

Since I don't know anything different, I wouldn't say I miss having a sense of smell. Most days I don't think about it. Of course, there are certain scents I would love to smell, even just once, such as a newborn baby, fresh-cut flowers, or a cinnamon bun (which I hear is awesome). But there are also lots of scents I'm happy never to have smelled. You can probably guess a few of those!

How does having no sense of smell affect my daily life?

I've learned how to live without a sense of smell. I'm careful when I'm cooking, though. I always set a timer because if I get distracted, a meal may end up burnt to a crisp before I know it. And I make sure my smoke detectors are always in working order. My nose won't warn me if there's a fire!

INDEX

A
adermatoglyphia 34–35
adrenaline 36
Alice in Wonderland
    Syndrome 22–23
amusia 14–15
amygdala 39
anosmia, congenital 38–39
auditory cortex 14

B
blood vessels 23, 29
brain cells 38

C
cilia 33, 38
cognitive maps 12
collagen 10
color 20, 21, 30, 31
color blindness 20–21
cone receptors 20
cornea 21

D
developmental topograph–
    ical disorientation 12–13
DNA 34
double–jointed 10–11
dreams 8, 9

E
earworm 15
emotional brain 39
endorphins 36
exploding head syndrome
    18–19
eye sockets 19, 32

eyes 8, 9, 13, 21, 22, 23,
    25, 29, 32

F
face blindness 24–25
fear 18, 36
feats of strength 36
fingerprints 34–35
fingers 10, 23, 34, 35

H
hair 28, 29
hands 10, 23, 29, 34–35
headache 22, 23, 31
heart 9, 19, 36
highly superior autobio–
    graphical memory 6–7
hippocampus 39
hyperdontia 26–27
hypodontia 26–27
hypothalamus 36

I
immune system 19
insomnia 18

J
joint hypermobility 10–11
joints 10, 11, 19, 36

L
lens 21
ligaments 10
limbic system 39
lobe, occipital 24, 22
lobe, temporal 22

M
medulla 33
memory 6, 7, 13, 14,
    19, 39
muscles 9, 19, 23, 33,
    36, 37
music 14, 15, 30

N
navigation 13
nerve endings, nerves 16,
    21, 23, 32, 33, 34
nerve, optic 21, 32
nerve, trigeminal 32
nervous system 36
nose 32, 33, 38, 39

O
olfactory bulb 39
olfactory system 38

P
photic sneeze syndrome
    32–33
photoreceptors 21
prefrontal cortex 6
prosopagnosia 24–25
pupil 21, 32

R
REM 9
retina 20

S
sensory sleep starts 18–19
sight, sense of 30

sleep 8, 9, 13, 18, 19, 22
sleep stages (cycles) 9
sleepwalking 8, 9
smell, sense of 17, 30,
    38, 39
sneeze 29, 32, 33
sun sneezing 32–33
supercolor vision 20–21
superior canal dehiscence
    syndrome 19
supernumerary teeth 26–27
super strength 36–37
supertasters 17
synesthesia 30–31

T
taste buds 16, 17
taste, sense of 16, 17, 30,
    31, 39
teeth 26, 27
tetrachromacy 20–21
tongue 23, 34, 16
touch, sense of 30, 34

U
uncombable hair syndrome
    28–29

V
vision 20, 21, 22, 29, 36

W
white matter 6, 14

TASTES LIKE MUSIC

ACKNOWLEDGMENTS:

A big thank you to the team at Owlkids, especially my insightful editors Jessica Burgess and John Crossingham, as well as Alisa Baldwin and Barb Kelly for your fantastic design. Thank you to Monika Melnychuk for your inspired artwork and to Dana Murchison for all the helpful comments. Sincere thanks to Alison Buckholtz, Nicole Donohue, Andrea Ray, Sharon Roseman, and Dr. Virginia Utermohlen for being so willing to share your stories with us. And, of course, a loving shout-out to Sam and Grace—my two most favorite people on the planet.

CONSULTANTS:

With much appreciation, I thank all of the experts who provided me with the research, information, and insights necessary to write this book:

Dr. Kirstie Anderson, Consultant Neurologist, RVI, Newcastle-upon-Tyne; **Dr. Patrick Arnold**, Pediatric Dentist; **Dr. Linda Bartoshuk**, Presidential Endowed Professor of Community Dentistry and Behavioral Science, University of Florida; **Dr. Michel Cramer Bornemann**, Departments of Neurology and Medicine, University of Minnesota Medical School and Department of Biomedical Engineering, University of Minnesota Graduate School, Twin Cities; **Dr. Bradley Duchaine**, Department of Psychological and Brain Sciences, Dartmouth College; **Dr. Rodney Grahame**, University College London Hospitals; **Dr. Veronica Gross**, Department of Psychology, Curry College; **Dr. Giuseppe Iaria**, Departments of Psychology and Clinical Neurosciences, University of Calgary; **Dr. Gabriele Jordan**, Institute of Neuroscience, Newcastle University; **Aurora LePort**, University of California, Irvine; **Dr. Roberta Pagon**, Department of Pediatrics, University of Washington; **Dr. Isabelle Peretz**, Département de psychologie, Université de Montréal; **Dr. Claudine Rieubland**, Department of Human Genetics, University of Bern; **Dr. Eli Sprecher**, Geneticist and Dermatologist, Tel Aviv Sourasky Medical Center, Israel; and **Dr. William Young**, Jefferson University Hospitals.